NAUSEA RHYMES

D.W. Briggs

I exist, that is all, and I find it nauseating.
Jean Paul Sartre

Published by New Generation Publishing in 2021

First Edition

ISBN: 978-1-80031-362-0

www.newgeneration-publishing.com

New Generation Publishing

FOREWORD

I am not a master of words; I am their lackey.
Great poets and balladeers have laid a table of eloquence and served a feast of powerful language. I am dishing up the leftovers, the crumbs, the scraps I found at the bottom of a foraging basket. Either you take them or you leave them.

If poetry is 'when an emotion has found its thought and the thought has found words'*, then maybe these poems have not yet found the poet.

Some of them I call songs. I have no musical talent, very little understanding of chords, scales and keys. Perhaps they have the meter of song lyrics, still searching for the music.

My drawings are idiosyncratic whims, not intending to decorate nor elucidate.

All in all,
I am just being myself and I am not going to apologise for it.

* Robert Frost

POEMS

LAUGHING LENNY 3

DO YOU GET THE DRIFT? 5

PRODIGAL SAVIOUR 9

BLIND MIRROR 15

THE INFUNDIBULAR POET 17

A PICTURE 21

FIRST POEM 25

THE SIXTH 27

MILTON'S DEPARTURE AND RETURN 31

DUR AND MOLL 35

NAUSEA RHYMES 39

SELF-MADE MAN 41

D.W. WHO? 45

HOLY HOLY HOLY 49

NOBODY TOLD ME 51

SONGS

BULLSHIT BROKERS 55

BIRDSONG NEMESIS 59

FRUIT CAN MAN BLUES 63

NO ESCAPE 67

BELIEVE ME 73

WIGGLE WAGGLE RAG 77

TIMELESS ENCOUNTER 81

POEMS

ww.ticket
OLD IDEAS
21:00 h.
INVITACIÓN
Prohibida su venta
Sector 104

LAUGHING LENNY

you lied to me when you were on speed
all that highbrow acid with backing vocals
you left me with a heap of broken images
piled up echoes of songs from a far-off room
a soggy blue raincoat hung up to dry
on a phony wooden tower
your innocence bewilders me

everybody is an asshole in some way or other
so why brag about it
remember when you were broke and broken
hallelujah for the casting show
crummy charlatan showman
so cool with your back-up gangster brides
practice made perfect with a happy end
your rehearsed duplicity makes me uncomfortable
not to worry—it is available on CD

I like your poetry
but I do not read it that often.

CITY LIGHTS
Ginsby boy, he's all over like horseshit
howling his dirty pome

DO YOU GET THE DRIFT?

beatniks
nix beat
beat up
upbeat confusion
dust and drag
drag and dust
and so on and so on
hanging their theories
on empty skies
empty skulls
discussing
howling
giving all
leaving nothing
so busy playing it cool
constantly opening doors
to visitations in the head
writing down a series of incidents
death hovering over
holy typewriters in
greenwich village

what does a beat poet do
at night
in nightmare land
indulging his ignorance
hiding his madness
under a burden of solitude
crawling through sewers
begging to buy excrement
shit so thick that words
cannot get through
defecating on society sidewalks
on streets renamed after beat poets
anywhere roads
so far out there is no way back
for the old
evil
and hungry
a frenzied few
amazing themselves
in a world too big
to contain multitudes

PRODIGAL SAVIOUR

A gargantuan and
voracious mollusc with
thousands of poisonous tentacles and
hundreds of gorgon-like heads
has risen up from stygian depths to
prey on the pure of heart and
turn the virtuous into stone.

Where are you, Perseus?
Where is your shiny shield?
Medusa has already left her
trilateral chambers along with
a clique of elite snakes in the grass and
is masquerading as world leaders
and Nobel Peace Prize winners.
She has been seen
alive and well in
Berlin, London, Tel-Aviv
and Washington,
with her serpent mane concealed
under a fashionable hat and
her vindictive eyes hidden
behind a mask of good will;
forever petrifying

unsuspecting onlookers and
spitting venom into the eyes of
innocent bystanders.

Where are you, Alethea?
The defender of
truth and sincerity
has deserted us,
left us to the mercy of the
masters of mass media.
On channel one,
hitman editors are
prompting newsroom sirens
to broadcast sophistry into
politically correct parlours.
On channel two,
chat show goblins are
stigmatising the forthright on
primetime pillories.
On channel three,
intellectual prostitutes are
licking the boots of the mammon,
betraying their principles and
selling their souls in return for
a chunk of daily bread.

Who do you think could redeem us?

The messiah went into retirement in
AD 33 and since then
has been claiming global superannuation.
Your esteemed Mr. Clean
got caught up in
a sticky web and was coerced into
swapping allegiances on
a first- class flight in mid-Atlantic.
Now he spends his time
out of sight and
beyond control,
throwing stones from
top floor windows of a
glass palace that belongs to
a non-transparent network, or
prowling in murky lobbies to
beguile avaricious politicians
in five-star hotel suites,
seducing with opportunities for
seats on the board,
business class miles
and more.

Who are you waiting for?
Our guardian angel lost his way
when his navigation system
redirected him to perdition,
via Geneva, Kyoto, Lima
and Paris,
and if he ever gets here
there will be nothing left
worth watching over.
Whilst we are sticking to
the old routine and
paying no attention to
what lies beyond the
tipping point of extinction,
our rainforests are being destroyed,
our drinking water polluted, and
our children poisoned in the womb.

Is there anybody left to deliver us from evil?
The good shepherd has lost his flock in
the wilderness of indifference.
The Light of the World has
reneged on millions of
displaced persons, crammed
into overcrowded camps in

Kenya, Jordan, South Sudan
and Tanzania.
In the dark and foul-smelling
alleyways of apathy
rats are multiplying fast and
feasting on the spoils of
refugee relief.
Demon puppets are dancing in
the streets of Damascus, Baghdad, Beirut
and Kabul,
and the princes of darkness are
pulling the strings.
Behind the scenes, billionaires are
stirring it up in cryptic kitchens,
whilst their vassals dish out
human suffering and depravation.
The Prince of Peace has
abandoned his disciples,
and armed with weapons of
mass destruction,
has joined the line of volunteers
for the unholy war.

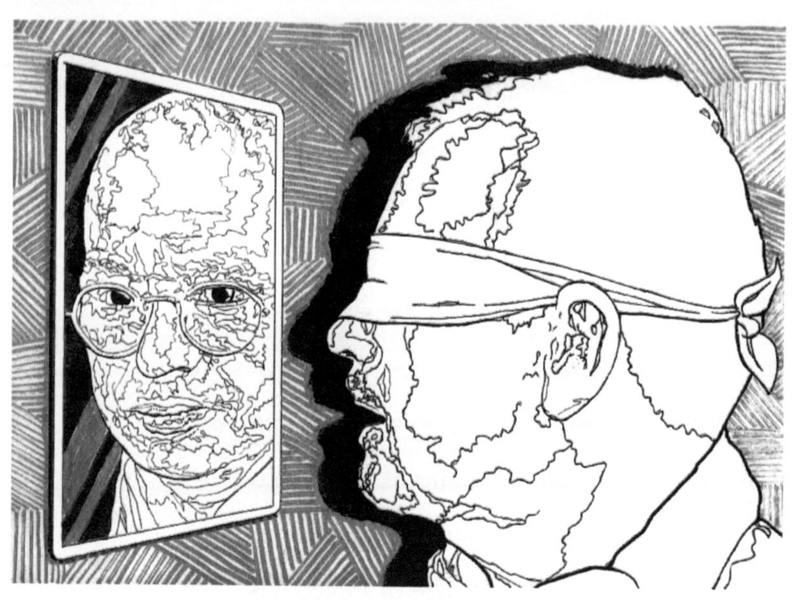

BLIND MIRROR

a

existence is a transitory illumination
between darkness and darkness
a blind mirror told me
a vivid dream for the duration
then eternal sleep is dreamless
a blind mirror showed me

our state after death
is the same as it was before birth
a blind mirror showed me
so before I draw my last breath
I will fill my life with mirth
just like the blind mirror told me

b

the only way to move a shite pile
is to shovel it
a blind mirror showed me
even though it takes a while
it will disappear shit by shit
a blind mirror told me

my head is full of excrement
my whole self is soiled and sordid
a blind mirror showed me
so before I receive my sacraments
I will refrain from being morbid
just like the blind mirror told me

THE INFUNDIBULAR POET

a born fool
        (pretends not to care)
tells song and dance stories
        (finds himself ridiculous)
lacks wisdom
        (lost in a clutter of information)
talks but he does not listen
        (afraid of forgetting what he wanted to say)
feels misunderstood
        (who could ever get wise to him?)
his memory torments him
        (beats him up on a daily basis)
pretends to be somebody
        (casts no shadow)
has no friends
        (meets up with strangers)
sees no light outside
        (darkness is within him)
makes a terrible mess of everything
        (cannot make up his mind)
is full of fear
        (his world has gone wrong)
wastes his time with philosophising
        (might just as well go insane)

scribbles fragments of thoughts on scraps of paper

(has lost the thread)

nibbles morsels of lyric poems

(regurgitates ragged rhymes)

his poetry is hollow

(the words in his vocabulary are too vacuous)

he is sick with idea deficiency

(muddled inconsistency)

he is dying for lack of words

(nothing will remain but scattered syllables)

A PICTURE

Mistakes were put down to immaturity by
shallow guardians of tender and impressionable youth,
seeing only themselves in
distorted reflection of chronic banality,
blind to the irreversible affliction caused by
negligent parental care.

Now that harm is done and
wounds cannot be healed,
a fading picture indicts those who
reneged on childhood dreams,
a portrait of a bleeding adult
cut by the jagged shards of a shattered childhood.

An accusing gaze looks straight through any
figment of self-reproach,
unforgiving eyes leave no question of guilt in
the observer's mind,
no right of appeal on
grounds of mitigating circumstances.

Such dark countenance,
a clean-cut mask slipped over a
washed-out spirit,

a wry smile with disdainful lips uttering
voiceless torments,
audible only in a bottled-up soul where
bitter dregs of cheap wine can
offer no solace or consolation.
While those who are accountable
jump over futile shadows to
embrace an illusion
in search of a broken bond with
offspring of a forlorn past
long since gone.

And in the end,
a tragic Wildean portrait
decomposes in an attic of guilt and regret,
the last remains of remorse
crumble to dust and
are whiffed away by
feeble sighs of resignation.

end

FIRST POEM

first I read
a long poem by
john dryden
(easy reading)
borrowed the word
beginning

then I read
a short poem by
robert creely
(hard going)
copied down the word
end

taking up my pen
I wrote my first poem

THE SIXTH

drunken insight
relieves me of rowdy revelry
the soul's mood seeks solitude
alone in forsaken walls
melancholia's refugium
in small hours

black vinyl
unsheathed
laid on a tawdry turntable
rotating
around its forlorn fulcrum
unworthy of its task
and then the low bassoon opens
violas appear
moving faster
spiralling
pulling down
into an inexorable vortex
yielding to pathetique's
four dark movements
                nightmarish loveliness
                disturbing desolation

bursting tension
anguished pain
concurrent suffering

pyotr ilyich's coffin
lies open
I stand in file
jesting with absent mourners
kiss his dead lips
bid his restless spirit farewell
to wander in the darkness
of contradictions
agony and extasy
passion and torment
bequeathing
total tragedy
unbearable intensity
until the finale
dying away

andante
sober
abandoned

J
J

MILTON'S DEPARTURE AND RETURN

In search of the sublime,
he juggles with rhyme.
His attempts to express
end up in a mess.
To free himself of this bondage,
he writes in ancient Greek language,
applying poetic ornament
to say what he meant.
At Homer's pleasure,
Virgil's Latin as measure,
the poet rejects vulgar rhyming,
wretched matter, lame timing.

The godly gods we must sanctify
the learned ancients say,
but to the devil we make sacrifice
if the modern poet has his way.
The trivialities of a barbarous age
bring forth bigotry and self-gainsay,
England's greatest poet and sage
his own words doth betray.
Thus, we wrestle with his language,

a choice of either sense or sound,
the monotony of his verse
our enjoyment doth confound.

Paradox lost, paradox regained.
What need'st thou, my Milton,
such weak witness of thy name?

KLARA GOLDSTEIN
PETR
KIND
644
581
29
D652
HAMBURG
D2
KÖLN 663

DUR AND MOLL

soprano with shaven scalp
maestro in prison rags
the pianist's hands are broken
the baritone is gagged
choir forever silenced
tenor shot in the head
chorus line decimated
the choreographer is dead

a morning raga
blues in the afternoon
an aria at sunset
sonata under the moon
screams are never silent
gunshots are always loud
the torturer is bragging
the mass murderer is proud

stroll along the shoreline
lakes and mountains
a walk in the park
flowers and fountains
an iron gate and railway lines

barbed wire and guards
the air is thick and greasy
the ground is bare and charred

conjure up emotion
passions swell and surge
the composer can't make up his mind
rhapsody or dirge
there is no dur there is no moll
no major or minor too
only stacked up suitcases
just a pile of shoes

J
J
J
J

ITY AGENCY
31,9225
31,946381
31,935328

NAUSEA RHYMES

The owl and the pussycat went to sea
In a rusty old oil tanker;
It went aground and now they found
Black oil spill on the Costa Blanca.

Little Bo Peep will rob your sleep,
Your personal data she will find it;
Leave her alone and she will tap your phone,
And you will not know who is behind it.

Jack and Jill cannot pay their bills,
So they cut off the power and water;
Jack went berserk and shot the utilities clerk,
So they jailed him forever after.

Hey diddle diddle, the minister's on the fiddle,
Expenses well over the moon;
The MPs laughed all the way to the bank,
Their next pay rise is coming up soon.

There was a crooked man and he lived a crooked life,
He founded a crooked NGO and took a crooked wife;
He bought a crooked politician who bought some crooked votes,
And the all lived together in the same crooked boat.

(Little Jack Horner)
Little Jack President sat in his residence
Dictating a pack of lies;
He stuck up his thumb to the applause of the dumb,
And said what a good guy am I.

AMOR ET NOGET

SELF-MADE MAN

nineteen sixty-five

london southwest five

smoking black sobranie

drinking screwdrivers

eating green noodles

piaf and greco

chanson with hands

hugues aufray chante dylan

the aussie barmaid

smiles at me

she can quote kerouac

and ginsberg

I tell her short-legged lies

propped up by

fake bohème

two thousand and fifteen

old wrinkled hands

mute postures

feuilles morte

a croaking bard

whose bottles are done

has killed each one

kerouac has gone down

the road
ginsberg's mirror
is empty
wasting time
manufacturing myths
playing biographical charades
in platitude boltholes
ashamed of shortcomings
nailed daily to
a cross of
contradictions
back to front
waiting in
no structural order
for the
inevitable
to happen
I can't remember the
barmaid's name

D.W. WHO?

All those winsome images,
momentous middle of the night inspirations,
fallen flat
in morning's rude awakening,
beyond reach
of artistry
never acquired.

All those lines
never written;
not one syllable
to be remembered by;
no redeeming peace
in my lack
of words.

I wanted to tell
so much
about despair
and how life must go on;
to write something
that need not
be explained.

Burnt up eloquence,
inarticulate ash,
doubts and confusions,
failure's furies turned loose,
screaming at me from barren pages;
while wordless poetry
was raging in
my soul.

I looked inside myself
but there was nothing in there
worth
writing about;
my inner sight purblind,
I could not find
the way
to reach
my heart.

So, I read
some stuff from Dylan Thomas
and Brendan Behan,
got drunk
and pretended to be a poet,
wrote naught
and talked
a lot.

HOLY HOLY HOLY

Holy orders

    Holy vows

Holy water

    Holy cow

Holy ghost

    Holy cloak

Holy Joe

    Holy smoke

Holy inquisitor

    Holy saviour

Holy Adolf

    Holy Eva

Holy believer

    Holy gentile

Holy deceiver

    Holy paedophile

Holy piss

    Holy crap

Holy this

    Holy that

Holy moly

    Every goddam thing is holy

NOBODY TOLD ME

I should have known better;
from the beginning
it was bound to come to nothing;
should have known
I wouldn't get far
but I was young and
nobody told me.

I wanted to shout,
shout out loud
but I could not even
whisper.
Words, too weak for the tongue,
stayed unspoken upon
my breath.

I knew what I wanted to say
but there was
too little of it,
not enough voice to
determine the
nature of
the sound.

Youth's noble dreams
vanquished and
melted down,
poured into mundane moulds
to be worn
as tarnished medals
on manhood's extended chest.

It was a mistake to
venture out on the quest for
self-discovery.
Now, I cannot find
the way back;
I am lost and running behind time.
Somebody should have told me.

SONGS

BULLSHIT BROKERS

If you want to know a man, give him power over you
You who follow the leader will dead end in a crash
Expect no mercy where brutality rules
And democracy is being traded in for cash

Siren server billionaires squander their sordid load
Destitution with no franchise continues to increase
Compassion, decency and dignity have no abode
And where hunger dwells there can be no peace

With nothing in their bellies
But with machetes in their hands
When there are no more trees to fell
They will cut down what they can

Court jesters play media mischief until the votes are cast
Complacency and blindness will take you for a fool
He who fools himself will not be laughing last
Hoodwinked by fast internet and social media drool

Virtual reality is cool and affordable
The real world is out
Hideous is restyled adorable
Dubious redefined as devout

The brokers of Ballyhoo
Spread their bullshit where you tread
Peddling their stinking brew
To contaminate your head

You can follow your own conviction
Or take the easy course
Do business with vendors of fiction
In empty outlets of guilt and remorse

Strike out, turn around, and go the other way
Take no heed of lowdown lunatics
Do your own thing no matter what they say
Don’t fall for their double-dealing tricks

If you want to know a man, give him power over you
You who follow the leader will dead end in a crash
Expect no mercy where brutality rules
And democracy is being traded in for cash

J
J

BIRDSONG NEMESIS

I'm not your friend, you're not my brother
Your fight for freedom doesn't make me free
When freedom's flame is smothered
It's too late to sing your songs of liberty
Your chorus asunder
Like birds on a tree
Singing one to another
They're not singing to me

I can make it through the day
In the night time, there is danger
So I had best be on my way
Before daylight to dark night changes
When tomorrow comes, it will be today
Time restarts and rearranges
Tomorrow when we meet again
We will meet as complete strangers

You can give your love to someone
Even though they don't return it
But you can't share friendship with anyone
Who coldheartedly spurns it
You can't undo the wrong you've done

Or throw it into the fire and burn it
They are not handing out a free pardon
You are going to have to earn it

A threshold you once did not cross
You cannot go over twice
If you enter Eden's gate by force
You will have to pay the price
If you storm the walls, no matter the loss
The falling stones, like rolling dice
Will come to rest and gather moss
At the gates of fool's paradise

You can hide away from life
But you can't escape from death
You can explain existence so precise
Until you breathe your very last breath
You are going nowhere and when you arrive
You'll have no more explanations left
Meaningless words will be your demise
And the measure of your success

Inside of me there's nothing wrong
That could not be put right
It's just that I do not belong
In the bad mad world outside
It has been in a mess for so long

Since fantasy first took flight
But it's the discord of the birdsong
That makes me tremble with fright

Their warbling has become absurd
The mocking bird will take his vengeance
The dawn chorus will be overheard
In a cacophony of violence
If you want to hear the songbird
You must listen to the silence
Broken only by a cry unheard
Since it was called out in the distance

To watch your world go under
Does not mean a thing to me
Confusion, default and blunder
Is all that I can see
Your chorus asunder
Like birds on a tree
Singing one to another
They're not singing to me

slices
TIN CAN PRESIDENT
TIN CAN MAN of the year

FRUIT CAN MAN BLUES

The pineapples are juicy, the peaches are sweet
The pineapples are juicy, the peaches are sweet
Pedro Pinoy is dying on his feet

Pedro and his family worked the land
Pedro and his family worked the land
Now they are the slaves of the fruit can man
They told Pedro to get off their land
They told Pedro to get off their land
The Government gave the land to the fruit can man

Pedro cried, 'I can't leave so quick'
Pedro cried, 'I can't leave so quick,
I got no money and my kids are sick'
You get out now or you'll regret it
You get out now or you'll regret it
Compensation, just forget it

Your fruit's not worth picking and your crops brings no yield
Your fruit's not worth picking and your crops brings no yield
We're planting more pineapple, we need more fields
They came with machetes and forced Pedro off the land
They came with machetes and forced Pedro off the land
Said, 'Report to the agent of the fruit can man'

You can work on the plantation, you can sleep here on the floor
You can work on the plantation, you can sleep here on the floor
You can buy dried fish and rice from the company store
We pay less than the legal working wage
We pay less than the legal working wage
If you complain, you can go on your way

Pedro can't pay the doctor, too many mouths to fill
Pedro can't pay the doctor, too many mouths to fill
Been buying from the store and he's run up a bill
Pedro's wife and kids are hungry, there's nothing left to eat
Pedro's wife and kids are hungry, there's nothing left to eat
Fruit can man sits in his villa drinking wine and eating meat

Think of peaches for a dollar, pineapple special price
A can of peaches for a dollar, pineapple special price
Think of Pedro Pinoy and then think twice

NO ESCAPE
For Haywood Patterson

This is the story of Haywood Patterson
Put on trial with no lawful defence
He suffered for a crime of which he was innocent
Condemned to prison with a life sentence

1931, Paint Rock, Alabama
Young hoboes riding a freight train
The white boys caused the trouble
The black boys got the blame

They took them to Scottsboro courthouse
Outside there was an ugly crowd
Accused of rape by two white women
Witnesses were quickly found

The women were of low repute
Their testimonies did not coincide
The police said, 'Accuse the negro boys
You are white, nobody will say you lied'

There was no evidence to support the indictment
One of the women said, 'Nobody raped me'
But in Alabama, just one woman's say was enough
And the all-white jury agreed

Eight teenage boys were convicted
To die on the electric chair
Denied their rights of counsel
Judge Hawkins didn't care

There were protest parades in Washington
Demonstrations in Berlin
The Scottsboro defence committee's
Monthly sum was coming in

But the governor's office door was closed
President Roosevelt was not at home
Though there was no case against them
The goddam negroes must atone

The Supreme Court spoke of injustice
The death sentence was reduced
They were all sent to prison camps
To be persecuted and abused

Haywood Patterson got seventy-five years
Four times he was on trial
No reprieve for the sonofabitch
For his guilt there can be no denial

In Atmore Prison, he was full of shame
But there could be no remorse
For the beatings, knives and gal boys
And some things that were worse

Confined in the terror of prison hell
He fought tooth and nail
They stabbed him to the brink of death
But death was better than Atmore Jail

Prison hard, afraid of nothing and nobody
He kept deadly snakes in his cell just for fun
Black snakes crawling over his black body
He was a devil and feared by everyone

After sixteen years in state prisons
Enduring brutality and hate
He decided enough was enough
And finally planned his escape

The Scottsboro Boy, he broke out
Now his terrible story has been told
But with the passing of time the interest
In the miscarriage of justice will grow cold

Haywood Patterson is on the run
But he will not get away
They will hunt him down and bring him back
And he will die in prison one day

J
J
J
J

BELIEVE ME

Don't say hello when we meet
I'll pretend I didn't see you
Look at my feet
And fasten my shoe
Till you've gone out of view

Don't message me on Facebook
No SMS nor email please
I just can't stand the look
Of you saying cheese
So don't post me anymore selfies

You showed me up in front of my friends
When you tweeted you will always love me
So this is where our relationship ends
I really mean it, believe me

Can do without your pettiness
All those trivial wasted tales
Coz I really couldn't care less
What the small talk entails
So spare me the chat lingo details

I have deleted my Instagram profile

No more on show in a goldfish bowl

Going to live in website exile

No more transmission protocol control

In my own internet black hole

You showed me up in front of my friends

When you tweeted you will never leave me

So this is where our relationship ends

And that's my last word, believe me

wriggle wagg
its the dis
zig
syncopate

WIGGLE WAGGLE RAG

Build it up, then bomb to the ground
Build again and blast it down
Say you are sorry, then do the same
Have fun playing the war game

Fool around with human strife
Toy with innocent peoples' lives
Little boys like to play with guns
Collateral damage can't spoil the fun

Syncopate that saxophone
Blow that cool trombone
Waggle wiggle wag
It's the discombobulated rag

Court jesters play their tricks
The name of the game is politics
Promises they always make
Are promises they're bound to break

And when all their solemn oaths are broken
A new false pledge is rashly spoken
It's common law for the common man
Money dictates the law of the land

Syncopate that saxophone
Blow that cool trombone
Waggle wiggle wag
It's the discombobulated rag

Work hard all your lives
Every day from eight till five
So the super-rich can live in style
Sitting pretty on top of the pile

Don't worry about your debts
The lender's interest rate is set
Do your job and do your best
To pay the compound interest

Syncopate that saxophone
Blow that cool trombone
Wiggle waggle wag
It's the discombobulated rag

Speculators dictate the rules of the game
Global players count their gains
Multinational companies, weapons, oil
Take control of foreign soil

Teddy Roosevelt is dead and gone
The robber barons still live on
They own the water, they own the fuel
Using bent governments to bend the rules

Syncopate that saxophone
Blow that cool trombone
Wiggle waggle wag
It's the discombobulated rag

They say our standard of living's in danger
From conspiracy theory troublemakers
Does nobody realise, no one have a clue
How the many are being controlled by the few

They've taken over, you have no choice
Democracy is dead, so let us all rejoice
Ringing in the end of the free world
As the Global Union flag unfurls

Syncopate that saxophone
Blow that cool trombone
Wiggle waggle wag
It's the discombobulated rag

Pray

TIMELESS ENCOUNTER

Alias and Alibi met on a winter's day
Says Alias to Alibi, 'Who are you, I pray?'
Says Alibi to Alias, 'It is not for me to say;
Don't ask silly questions, best be on your way'
And after they had spoken
And wasted not a word
It made no difference anyhow
To all that they had heard

Now the wind was getting colder
And it began to rain
So when they got tired of talking
They took shelter in a drain
Their camouflage cloaks were soaking wet
And their tongues began to freeze
Their teeth could not stop chattering
They were knocking at the knees

'I'm getting out of here', says Alibi
'This place is worse than hell.
I will take the road to heaven
Soon as the angels toll them bells'
'I hear no bells', says Alias

‘I can only hear the wails
Of those who must stay down here
And live to tell the tale’

After Alibi had parted
And was a long time gone
The souls that were remaining
Raised up their voices in a song
In praise of the Almighty
For opening up his home
To save that wretched traveller
Who had nowhere left to roam

The moral of this winter’s tale
The whole meaning of it all
Is that you can meet anyone by chance
No matter what they’re called
They came to this place from nowhere
Somewhere no one has seen
And they’re going back to the place
Where they have never been

They may tremble in their footsteps
Bang their heads against the wall
Invoke the hosts of heaven

Or heed the devil's call

Look back to the future

Or forward to the past

Eternity is the end of the line

When they breathe their last

AFTERWORD

Immature poets imitate, mature poets steal.

T.S. Eliot

If I have imitated, at least I have done something.

If I have stolen, I hope I did not heedlessly deface what I have taken by trying to do something different with it.

www.ingramcontent.com/pod-product-compliance
Ingram Content Group UK Ltd.
Pitfield, Milton Keynes, MK11 3LW, UK
UKHW041641190726
13854UKWH00006B/2640

9 781800 313620